SAN ANTONIO

TEXAS   A PHOTOGRAPHIC PORTRAIT

PHOTOGRAPHY BY **AL RENDON** | NARRATIVE BY **GARY S. WHITFORD**

TWIN LIGHTS PUBLISHERS | ROCKPORT, MASSACHUSETTS

TRAVIS

First published in the
United States of America by:

Twin Lights Publishers, Inc.
Rockport, Massachusetts 01966
Telephone: (978) 546-7398
www.twinlightspub.com

ISBN: 978-1-934907-48-1

10 9 8 7 6 5 4 3 2 1

(opposite)
The legendary stories of the Alamo battle
placed a handful of heroes in the pantheon of
American freedom fighters. Sculptor Pompeo
Coppini crafted this huge cenotaph on the
corner of Alamo Plaza in celebration of the
battle's centenary.

(frontispiece)
Mission San José

(jacket front)
Battle of the Alamo Reenactors

(jacket back)
River Walk and Mission Espada

Book design by:
SYP Design & Production, Inc.
www.sypdesign.com

Printed in China

CROCKETT

an Antonians gather at the river. For thousands of years, people have lived on the banks of what the Payayas called Yanaguana, refreshing waters. On June 13, 1691, Franciscan Fray Damian Massanet and Governor Domingo Terán de los Ríos, camped next to a Payayan village. Fr. Massanet wrote that clear water erupted from the earth in abundance. It was the feast day of San Antonio de Padua.

By 1718, Spanish missionaries and soldiers had established San Antonio de Valero, a mission and presidio that would become known as the Alamo. Amicable natives converted to Catholicism and adopted Spanish culture. In 1731, Canary Islanders arrived and established San Fernando de Béxar. Over the next 300 years, San Antonio would grow into the 7th most populated city in the United States and second-largest in Texas with 1.4 million people.

On March 6, 1836, Mexican troops finally prevailed against a stalwart force of Texans and American settlers at the Alamo after a 13-day siege and battle. The inspiring defense turned defeat into unforgettable legend. A few weeks later, Texas won its revolution in San Jacinto.

Throughout its history, San Antonio has attracted a diverse population. While Mexican-Americans comprise nearly 60 percent of the population and shaped the city's genesis, San Antonio was also formed by settlers from the East and Midwest and European immigrants—at one time, the majority of San Antonians spoke German.

San Antonio has always been a military city, and troops from every corner of the nation have been trained or served here. Many service members return to San Antonio when they retire. Everyone who comes brings another contribution to its character, and the city has become a vibrant multicultural community.

San Antonio is a city of education, medicine, defense, and trade. It's a religious city, praying to saints, and bonding with family. It is a border town, a city with its own distinctive blend of music, Tex-Mex food, art, and fiestas. The Alamo City is fiercely proud of its history and looking forward to a bright, sustainable future.

World's Largest Cowboy Boots (opposite)

Giant cowboy boots alongside the expressway kick up Texas spirit. In 1979, Bob Wade built the boots for a Washington, D.C. art festival. In1980 the sculpture was moved to its present, permanent location at North Star Mall. The Guinness Book of World Records listed the boots as the largest Cowboy Boot Sculpture.

Mission Espada *(above)*

The Southernmost San Antonio mission, Mission San Francisco de la Espada came to the San Antonio River area in 1731, transferred from an area near present-day Weches, Texas, where it was founded as Mission San Francisco de los Tejas in 1660.

Education & Work *(left and opposite)*

Edmundo Rios III demonstrates his roping skills in front of Mission Espada. Franciscan missionaries endeavored to teach Spanish Catholic culture and impressed natives with tools, clothing and skills, including agriculture, horsemanship, and construction. Trades and knowledge passed down through the generations helped build San Antonio.

Sharing Water

A well outside Mission San José is part of a 15-mile water system engineered by Spanish soldiers and missionaries and built by natives. Mission life offered Payaya natives education, food and clothing, and protection from Apache marauders.

Mission San José *(above and pages 10–11)*

High on a sacristy wall in the corner of Mission San José, the Rose Window casts reverence into the old church. The window is commonly thought to have been created by Pedro Huizar. Built in 1720, Mission San José was founded by Father Antonio Margil de Jesús, a prominent Franciscan.

Mission Concepción (top and opposite)

Mission Nuestra Señora de la Purísima Concepción de Acuña was transferred to the San Antonio area from its original location in East Texas in 1731, 15 years after its founding. Missionaries replaced indigenous rituals with Catholic sacraments and ceremonies. All four non-Alamo missions have active parishes and hold church services.

Frescoes (bottom)

Franciscan priests were educated in a variety of tasks, which they could use to bring Spanish Catholic culture to the "wild" hinterlands. The art of frescoes was part of that skill set, which they passed on to indigenous tribe members. This fresco depicts God as a mestizo.

Sacred Images *(left and right)*

Most of the missions had bright frescos painted inside and out. Weather has erased most of the exterior paintings, but solid construction and loving maintenance have preserved many of the interior frescos and carvings like these in Mission Concepción.

A Working Parish

For the monks, the most important function of the church is to support one's immortal soul. Symbolic art gives these aged walls a special power to rekindle and refresh faith. Visitors respect the sanctity of the missions, keeping voices low and respectful. Masses in the missions carry a legacy of worship.

Mission San Juan Capistrano

Sharing a name with a famous California mission, Mission San Juan Capistrano was transferred from East Texas and re-established along the San Antonio River in 1731. San Juan was a survivor, overcoming disease and attacks from the Apache and Comanche tribes. The mission provided protected huts, agriculture, and religious education.

Alamo

In 1716, the Mission San Antonio de Valero was established by Father Antonio de San Buenaventura y Olivares and relocated several times until reaching its current location. The Alamo is one of the most visited historic landmarks in America, site of a legendary battle in 1836.

Cenotaph

Stories of heroism among the defenders of the Alamo sanctified the site. "Remember the Alamo" became a rallying cry, and Texans give great respect to "The Shrine of Texas Liberty." In 1936, the Alamo battle centennial, the State of Texas commissioned sculptor Pompeo Coppini to create the *Spirit of Sacrifice*.

Celebration Central *(above and opposite)*

Located across the street from the River Walk in the heart of San Antonio, the Alamo is part of the celebrations and political gatherings throughout the year. Bill FitzGibbons "painted" the Alamo in colored light during an early "Luminarias" (Festival of Lights) art celebration.

Alamo Christmas Tree *(right)*

On the Friday after Thanksgiving, Alamo Plaza hosts the ceremony that ignites holiday lights on the Plaza, the River Walk, and throughout downtown San Antonio. A river boat parade and other events highlight the evening.

Alamo Reenactment *(above and left)*

Each year at the end of February through early March, the San Antonio Living History Association reenacts the events leading up to the March 6, 1836 Battle of the Alamo. Volunteers don historically correct clothing and carry vintage tools and weapons to represent the brave residents during the historic fight.

San Antonio's Original Melting Pot

The Alamo became the destination and temporary home for members of native tribes and many groups of immigrating Americans and Europeans. San Antonio was the center of commerce, defense, and industry in Texas from the establishment of the missions through the early 20th century.

Edward Steves Homestead

(opposite top and bottom)

The home of Edward Steves is one of several "house museums" in the King William Historical District, built in the 19th century by largely German immigrants. German doctors, merchants, builders, artisans, and educators came to the Texas Hill Country to establish a "utopia" of democracy and egalitarianism.

Edward Steves *(above)*

Edward Steves founded Steves Lumber in 1866. His firm imported Louisiana cypress and long-leaf Florida pine to South Texas. His son, Albert Steves Sr., was instrumental in the railroad business. The homestead was donated to the San Antonio Conservation Society in 1952.

Guenther House *(above and left)*

Carl H. Guenther immigrated to Texas in 1851, building a gristmill by hand in Fredericksburg, then established C.H. Guenther & Son in San Antonio. The Pioneer Flour Mill continues to supply bakers throughout the state, and the Guenther House is one of the distinguished house museums in King William.

Brunch at the Guenther House

The Guenther House hosts a fine restaurant, known for its all-day breakfast and lunch menu. Patrons can choose indoor seating or enjoy the fresh air on the patio. Afterwards they can tour the gracefully restored 1860 house, museum, and store.

Anton Wulff House *(above)*

Businessman Anton Wulff built the house at 107 King William in 1869. The house underwent a number of transformations through its history until the 1970s, when the San Antonio Conservation Society purchased the home and restored it to its 19th-century look with a U.S. Economic Development agency grant.

King William Cultural Arts District
(left and opposite)

The King William neighborhood has assembled a community of residents who treasure San Antonio's history and share a commitment to preserving historic structures and arts. The King William Cultural Arts District is the gateway to Southtown, featuring independent galleries, schools, breweries, and chef-directed restaurants.

Villa Finale *(opposite top and bottom)*

Merchant Russel Norton built this residence in 1876. The home went through a variety of travails and a succession of owners until conservationist Walter Nold Mathis renovated the home in 1967. Villa Finale, with Mathis' collections, became the only Texas site of the National Trust for Historic Preservation in 2004.

Lambermont *(above)*

Edwin Holland Terrell built the Alfred Giles-designed Lambermont, also known as "Terrell Castle," a few miles away from King William on Grayson Street. It housed the Terrell family until the ambassador's death in 1910. In 2008, Pat and Dona Liston purchased the historic site and renovated it for a popular event venue.

Spanish Governor's Palace

(above, left, and opposite)

The *Comandancia* remains the only example of colonial residential architecture in Texas. In 1928, the building was championed by conservationist Adina De Zavala and the Texas Historical and Landmark Association. The City of San Antonio purchased the building and it became known as "The Spanish Governor's Palace."

Spanish Governor's Palace

(above and left)

Built for representatives of the Spanish government, the Comandancia was dressed to house and welcome dignitaries. Imported furnishings of the finest materials provided requisite elegance. The Palace serves as a museum located across the street from a current seat of power, City Hall.

Pearl Stable

Founded by a group of investors in the 1880s, Pearl Brewery grew to be the largest brewery in Texas in the 1920s. Huge wagons drawn by draught horses distributed the beer throughout Texas and the nation. Today, it is a unique venue for social events.

Museum Reach

In 2009, the River Walk began expansions to the north and south of downtown. The north section, "Museum Reach" passes the San Antonio Museum of Art and the rapidly growing Pearl Brewery development. The Museum Reach features beautiful landscaping, a pedestrian bridge, lighting, and public art.

Pearl Brewery (above)

After three years of private ownership, the San Antonio Brewing Association purchased a fledgling microbrewery and modernized it with a new recipe by German master brewers. After the brewery closed, it became the site of a huge mixed-use revitalization with high-end restaurants, urban apartments, offices, and retail.

Pearl Turnaround (pages 38–39)

When the Museum Reach of the River Walk was built, a series of locks were required to help the famous river boats navigate the upper section. The boats turn around next to the Pearl Brewery community, delighting passengers and passers-by with the spectacle.

Riverwalk (opposite)

San Antonio's renowned River Walk is a canal built to channel the confluence of springs rolling toward the Gulf of Mexico that once flooded large parts of the city. Today, Casa Rio's iconic umbrellas attract visitors downstairs to food and fun.

Buzzing with Activity (above)

The Downtown Reach of the River Walk is lined with restaurants and shops. From Air Force trainees and their families to visiting sports fans to ordinary tourists, the River Walk keeps downtown vibrant. River boats loaded with visitors provide guided tours. Music flows as mariachis entertain diners.

Hugman Dam (*above*)

Left alone, the San Antonio River would not fill its canal except during flood-condition rains. A series of dams keeps the level up and flowing through downtown. This dam is named for Robert H.H. Hugman, a visionary architect who drew plans for the River Walk in the 1930s.

Fowl of a Feather

(*right, opposite, and pages 44–45*)

No species enjoys a lush garden surrounded river like our fine-feathered friends. Ducks proliferate, and despite requests otherwise, receive tidbits from walkers and diners. Other parts of the River Walk, such as the Mission Reach, see herons, cranes, songbirds, bats, owls, and other flying species.

Riverwalk Mission Reach

(above and opposite top)

The Mission Reach is an eight-mile stretch south of downtown that passes four of the historic 18th-century missions. The wide paved "trail" is open to walkers, joggers, and bikes. Freshly landscaped with native flora, migrating waterfowl can be seen and wildflowers blossom along the path through the spring.

Texas State Flower (*right*)

Seeded in the fall, the bluebonnet germinates through the winter and then rises from the soil in the spring all over the Texas Hill Country. Many families maintain a tradition each year of "bluebonnet pictures," photos of their children, from confused babies to reluctant teens.

Fort Sam Houston *(top and bottom)*

The site of the first military flight, "Fort Sam" is part of Joint Base San Antonio and the home of the San Antonio Military Medical Center. JBSA is under the command of the 502d Air Base Wing, which also operates Randolph and Lackland AFB facilities.

Fort Sam Houston Museum *(opposite)*

One of the oldest military installations in the United States, Fort Sam Houston is a National Historic Landmark with more than 900 historic structures, including the famous quadrangle. The Fort Sam Houston Museum covers the fort's storied history.

U.S. Army Medical Museum

Fort Sam Houston has trained medics for more than a century, and today serves as home to the San Antonio Military Medical Center, training and caring for members of all the armed forces. The Army Medical Museum teaches the history of U.S. military medical teams.

"Medic!" *(top and bottom)*

The casualties of war make the unit medic an important part of every mission. Medics save lives and limbs. Medical solutions in combat often produce innovations that contribute to civilian medicine, helping prevent infection, improve trauma response, and facilitate recovery.

San Antonio Fire Museum

(above and left)

America was once built of very flammable wood. A single spark could ignite an entire city. Firefighters are true heroes. Housed on the site of the first fire house in the city, the San Antonio Fire Museum honors heroes and technology that save lives and property every day.

Saving the City (above and right)

Long ago, when the city was made of adobe and wood, volunteers rallied to the sound of church bells, rushing in to extinguish the fire. In 1891, fire fighting technology and building materials led to a professional force, no less brave and very effective.

Texas Transportation Museum

(above and left)

Texas connects to the world with roadways, railways, and flight paths. The vehicles that travel those trails have driven commerce since people inhabited the state. Railroads represent a significant part of that heritage. Volunteers have collected, restored, and operate a variety of vehicles at the Texas Transportation Museum.

All Aboard *(opposite top and bottom)*

The Texas Transportation Museum offers a robust educational experience, including scheduled rides on the Longhorn & Western Railroad on the weekends. The museum's collection of rolling stock includes engines, passenger cars, motor railcars, and cabooses. You can also see horse carriages, automobiles, tractors, and model trains.

Tobin Center

San Antonio's premier performances stage at Tobin Center for the Performing Arts. Built in 1926 as Municipal Auditorium, the venue was fully expanded and given an acoustic makeover in 2014. The Tobin, named after arts champion Robert L.B. Tobin, is the home of the San Antonio Symphony.

McNay Art Museum *(above and right)*

Heiress Marian Koogler McNay came to San Antonio in 1926. She commissioned a Spanish colonial-revival house and began collecting modern art. McNay bequeathed her estate and an endowment to establish the first modern art museum in Texas. The stainless steel sculpture (lower right) is *Victoria* by Phillip Grausman.

Stieren Center for Exhibitions *(above)*

In 2008, the McNay doubled its exhibition space with the Stieren Center. The Brown Sculpture Terrace is in front of the building, including Barbara Hepburn's *Cantate Domino*, which is part of the McNay Art Museum Collection and a gift of the estate of Tom Slick.

Blackburn Patio *(opposite)*

The Blackburn Patio is nature's art complementing the exhibitions inside. The McNay has inspired several generations of San Antonians with its collection of paintings, sculptures, prints, and photographs representing medieval to 21st-century European and American cultures, the Tobin Collection of Theatre Arts and more.

San Antonio Museum of Art

In 1981, the San Antonio Museum Association opened the San Antonio Museum of Art in a beautiful renovation of the historic Lone Star Brewery. From a collection of American, Pre-Columbian and Latin art begun in the 1920s, SAMA has grown to represent a broad range of cultures and eras.

Cowboys and Indians

The art of the American West is a lot more than paintings of cowboys on horseback. Located downtown on the River Walk and named for former governor Dolph Briscoe and his wife, Janey, the Briscoe Western Art Museum has an extensive collection of Native American art, sculpture, photography, literature, and classic paintings.

DoSeum (above)

San Antonio's DoSeum encourages children to exercise their minds and bodies with an interactive robot named Baxter, a spy academy with math challenges, interactive puppet parade, musical staircase, accessible treehouse, and a Children's River. The DoSeum is a few blocks south of the Witte Museum on Broadway.

Prarie Grass Sculpture (left)

Beth Galston's *Prairie Grass* is a kinetic sculpture greeting visitors to the city's Northwest Service Center. Visitors can walk through the sculpture, which captures the spirit of wind rippling the tall grasses that once covered Texas and fed millions of bison.

Open Hand, Open Heart, Open Mind (opposite)

A large open hand rises from Pittman-Sullivan Park on the East side of San Antonio overlooking the downtown skyline. Based on the writings of Martin Luther King, Jr., the interactive sculpture by Douglas Kornfeld stands at the destination point for San Antonio's MLK Day March.

Buckhorn Saloon & Museum

Visitors come to Texas to see the Old West. For 131 years, the Buckhorn Saloon has served thirsty visitors in style. Famous for hunting trophies and artifacts, the buckhorn has a saloon, a shooting gallery, and, of course, a gift shop.

A Historic City Center

At one time the scene of chili queens and gunfights, the streets of today's downtown San Antonio are full of history and character. Horse-drawn carriages and tour buses carry visitors past the Alamo, the Buckhorn, historic Menger Hotel, museums, parks, theaters, and other attractions.

El Mercado

El Mercado, or Market Square is a
collection of shops and restaurants
featuring Mexican clothing, pottery,
curios, and other wonders. City
celebrations are held in the large
courtyard, and the Mercado is always
buzzing with activity. It's a colorful,
chaotic, exciting scene that should
not be missed.

Mi Tierra

San Antonio attracts people interested in Mexican culture, shopping and "Tex-Mex" cuisine. Visitors flock to El Mercado and Mi Tierra, perhaps the city's most famous restaurant. Open 24 hours, the restaurant offers "Mexican Food" favorites, live mariachis, and a panaderia – a bakery with empanadas, pan dulce, and other treats.

American Dream

For 25 years, La Familia Cortez, owners of Mi Tierra, have commissioned a continuing mural. The huge canvas features more than 200 prominent San Antonians, adding new figures as they emerge in politics, the arts, or community service. To date, five artists have contributed to the mural.

Fig Tree Restaurant (top)

Two historic restaurants line the River Walk edge of La Villita—Fig Tree and Little Rhein Steakhouse. The Fig Tree is located in the Gray-Guilbeau House, built in 1847. The building was the last residence occupied in La Villita, with the final owners—the Phelps family—founding Fig Tree.

Little Rhein (bottom)

You don't "belly up to the bar" at Little Rhein Steakhouse, but for the Old West staples of steak and whisky, it's your destination of choice. La Villita began in the 1500s as a Coahuiltecan native village. Later, German immigrants called the neighborhood "Little Rhein," which gave the steakhouse its name.

Evening in San Antonio

As a city of landmarks, San Antonio has grown with a careful eye on history. Conservation is a significant value, and our architecture creates a distinctive, unique appearance. The lights on the buildings, along the River Walk, and around the plazas define urban beauty.

The Grotto (above and left)

Three generations of Cortés artists have created faux bois sculptures that shape concrete to look like wood. Carlos Cortés created this three-story Grotto for the Museum Reach. It features carved faces and other entertaining details, as well as seating and a stairway that passes through a huge jaguar's open mouth.

F.I.S.H. (opposite)

Not all of the fish in the San Antonio River are in the water. Donald Lipski's *F.I.S.H.* is an installation of sunfish (native to the river) enlarged "Texas-sized" and arranged under an overpass. Strollers on the Museum Reach encounter the sculpture and then come back to see it in its evening glory.

Sunset Station (above)

The Southern Pacific Terminal in St. Paul Square has become a large dining and entertainment venue. The Sunset Limited is a famous train in the Amtrak network, traveling from Florida to Arizona. Sunset Station has become an after-work oasis of fun and refreshment. Amtrak maintains an active depot behind the restaurant.

Tower Life Building (left)

Built in 1927, the 30-story Ayres & Ayres designed building has a terracotta tower complete with gargoyles. Lit every night, the building was registered on the National Register of Historic Places in 1991.

Tower of the Americas (opposite)

In 1968, San Antonio's hosted Hemis-Fair, a year-long exposition. Designed by renowned architect O'Neil Ford, a 750-foot revolving restaurant and observation tower instantly became the identifying feature on the skyline and a natural backdrop for New Year's and Independence Day fireworks.

Dressed for the Holidays *(top)*

River Walk boats become parade floats during Fiesta and the Christmas holidays. Downtown is dressed for the season with thousands of colored lights, most concentrated along the Downtown Reach of the river. The Holiday River Parade travels the route on the Friday after Thanksgiving, with bands, carolers, and Santa.

Glitz and Glitter *(bottom)*

Holidays are concentrated in December as humanity combats the darkness of winter with bright lights and prayers for peace. San Antonio's streets and buildings take on a jolly spirit. It's a most wonderful time of the year in the Alamo City.

Songs of the Season

(opposite and pages 78-79)

Every evening between the end of November and Christmas, local church and school choirs board barges and float down the river singing carols and spreading cheer. Accommodating weather calls visitors to have a meal, do some shopping, and create lifetime memories..

Emily Morgan Hotel *(opposite)*

Located on Houston Street, the Emily Morgan Hotel is named for Emily West, a heroine of the Texas Revolution. Ms. Morgan is reputed to be the legendary siren that distracted Santa Anna during the Battle of San Jacinto, a conflict between Spanish troops and Sam Houston's Texans that ended the war.

Bexar County Courthouse *(above)*

Constructed 1892–1897, the temple-like building is the largest and oldest continually operating courthouse in Texas. Bexar County is the fifth seat of government to reside in the location, which also served Spain, Mexico, the Republic of Texas, the Confederate States, and U.S. federal offices. It is listed on 11 historic registers.

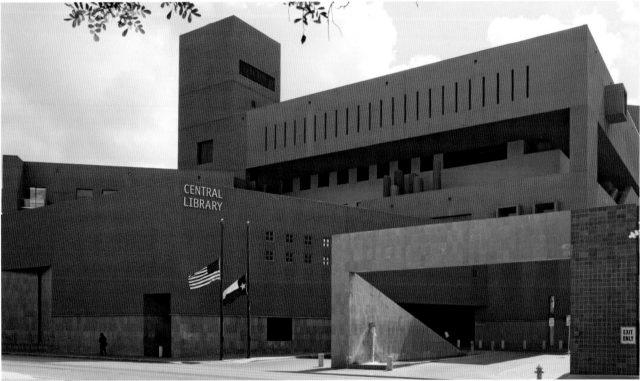

Gonzalez Convention Center
(top and opposite)

Named for a popular congressman, the Henry B. Gonzalez Convention Center opened with HemisFair in 1968 and has been renovated several times. The center hosts more than 300 events annually with more than 750,000 delegates. The River Walk has a spur that wends through the convention center.

Central Library *(bottom)*

In 1995, San Antonio's Central Library, the cornerstone of a 29-branch system and portal, opened at the site of a Sears, Roebuck & Co. store. The "Enchilada Red" Mexican Modernist architecture immediately attracted national note, and the Library is a popular downtown oasis.

Mays Family Center (top)

A massive 10,000–square-foot exhibition space facilitates "blockbuster" events for the historic Witte Museum of Science & Natural History. Dinosaur footprints adorn the façade, and the center sits on a portion of the Acequia Madre, the aqueduct system that once distributed water for the Alamo and the 18th-century missions.

Witte Museum (bottom)

Generations have learned about their history and natural environment at the Whitte Museum. Led by a teacher, the museum was established in the 1920s by a civic effort that included children selling bluebonnets and cakes. The South Texas Heritage Center houses rare artifacts and documents of San Antonio's rich history.

Friendship Torch (opposite)

Sebastián's La Antorcha de la Amistad (Torch of Friendship) commemorates the 500-year connection between San Antonio and Mexico. Commissioned by the Asociación de Empresarios Mexicanos (Mexican entrepreneurs), La Antorcha was erected in 2002. Just 150 miles from the Mexican border, San Antonio is a major gateway to international trade.

Majestic Theatre *(top)*

One by one, San Antonio has renovated and restored several of its classic theatres. The Majestic is the queen of that effort. Built in 1929, the ornate Spanish Mediterranean design continues from the marquee into the theatre, with a faux night sky and gilded decoration, topped off by Greco-Roman sculptures.

Alameda Theatre *(left)*

When it opened in 1949, the Alameda Theatre was the largest movie palace ever dedicated to Spanish language films and performing arts. Located on the near edge of the Westside barrios, it remains an important icon of Mexican-American culture.

Empire Theatre *(top)*

The Majestic's sister theatre, the Charline McCombs Empire is the scene of many road shows visiting San Antonio, from jazz to comedians to dance performances. Built in 1913 on the site of an opera house, it was restored by Las Casas Foundation and reopened in 1998.

Mission Drive-In Theatre *(right)*

All that's left of San Antonio's last vintage drive-in theatre is its restored marquee, facing Roosevelt Street on the way to the missions. The 26-acre site was once hunting grounds for Coahuiltecan natives and agricultural land tilled by the nearby San José Mission.

City Skyline *(pages 88–89)*

Looking southeast from the northern edge of downtown, some of San Antonio's iconic landmarks present their best face. From left, Rivercenter Mall, La Antorcha de Amistad, the Convention Center, Tower of the Americas, and the Palacio del Rio; River Walk trees are in the foreground.

Market Square

Famous as "the largest Mexican market outside Mexico," Market Square (El Mercado) has 100 locally owned shops offering bakery items, pottery, and curios. It is the city's primary celebration site, with numerous annual festivals and gatherings. For most of its history, the square was also home to farmers offering fresh produce.

Carriage Rides

You could zip down Alamo Street past the Alamo, around La Villita, over the River Walk and pass right by dozens of historic landmarks or you could park, board a decorated horse-drawn carriage and really see this beautiful town. Carriage rides delight your princess and ease your queen's aching feet.

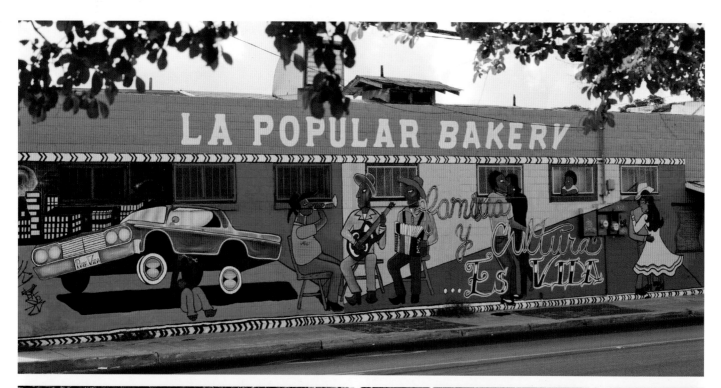

Westside Murals (top and bottom)

Stretching back to pre-Columbian Aztecs and other indigenous cultures, artists have always expressed their religious, political, and aesthetic vision with monumental paintings. In recent years, the San Anto Cultural Arts organization has organized a return to the tradition of restoring and commissioning murals that project today's culture and values.

Spirit of Healing

Internationally known artist Jesse Treviño painted this nine-story mural on Christus Santa Rosa Children's Hospital. "The dove represents the spirit of life," Treviño said, "We must take care that children are taken care of."

Laredito

Jesse Treviño painted ceramic tiles to reproduce the ambience of a popular Westside neighborhood for a mural at the Casa Navarro State Historic Park. Laredito (Little Laredo) was a hotspot of culture with family gatherings, music, and food.

Casa Navarro

José Antonio Navarro was a hero of the Texas Revolution, rancher, and businessman. A member of Spanish viceroyalty, he was also a self-educated attorney and collaborated with Stephen F. Austin in bringing settlers to Texas. His home in San Antonio is a state historic site.

Espada Aqueduct *(above and left)*

The benefits of a steady, clear river were distributed to the fledgling missions growing near the San Antonio River by a system of dams and acequias. From 1731–1745, Franciscan friars led the construction of the acequia that reached Mission Espada. A portion of that important waterway remains in the Missions National Park.

Texas Longhorn *(opposite)*

Texas's reputation for growing everything large may thank Longhorn cattle, a breed mixed from Spanish stock brought to the state in the 17th century and British Bakewell stock from the Midwest in the 1820s. By the time Longhorns reach four years old, their horns can extend 5.9 feet.

San Pedro Park Pool *(above)*

A tributary feeding the San Antonio River, San Pedro Creek attracted indigenous tribes and settlers to its banks. The park was the scene for Sunday gatherings in the 19th century, where shade and a pond at the source of the creek provided welcome relief. Today, it's one of the city's prettiest swimming pools.

Natural Bridge Caverns *(left)*

The largest commercial cave system in Texas is named for a 60-foot-span created when a sinkhole dropped out from under a rock formation. In 1960, four St. Mary's University students discovered a large cave now known as the "north cavern." Further exploration extended the initial space over several miles.

San Pedro Park

Texas' oldest designated park is a 46-acre greenspace that hosts a library, tennis center, theater, pool, playgrounds, and picnic area. In 1854, John J. Duerler, a Swiss landscape designer, purchased and leased land around the San Pedro Springs, built improvements, and planted tropical flora.

Institute of Texan Cultures *(top)*

The Institute of Texan Cultures building was constructed for the 1968 Hemis-Fair, serving as the Texas Pavilion. After the fair, the facility became a museum and library, and sponsors the annual Texas Folklife Festival celebrating the myriad ethnicities that contribute to the city's culture. ITC is currently operated by UTSA.

HemisFair Park Fountains

(above and opposite bottom)

One of HemisFair's most popular remnants, large fountains invite visitors to stroll under their mist and sit beside cascading waterfalls. The fountains were turned off sometime in the early 21st century. In 2010, they were retrofitted to use alluvial reclaimed water and flow once more.

Brackenridge Eagle

Built in 1956, the Brackenridge Eagle
miniature train was once the longest
miniature railroad in the world. Now
known as the San Antonio Zoo Eagle,
the train course connects the zoo
with the Witte Museum, Kiddie Park,
and the Japanese Tea Garden. It
crosses the river and passes through
lovely woods.

Brackenridge Golf Course

(top and bottom)

George W. Brackenridge was a cotton merchant and became a major philanthropist. The Brackenridge estate extended from Pearl Brewery to University of the Incarnate Word and the source of the San Antonio River. Brackenridge maintained a habitat for exotic animals where golfers play today.

Japanese Tea Garden *(opposite)*

Also known as Sunken Gardens, the Japanese Tea Garden was built into an abandoned quarry that once contributed to many historic buildings, including the Menger Hotel. In 1918, using donated funds and prison labor, parks commissioner Ray Lambert directed construction of pathways, gardening beds, stone bridges, and a Japanese pagoda.

San Antonio Botanical Garden *(above)*

Less than two miles east of the Japanese Tea Garden, the San Antonio Botanical Garden is a series of display and formal gardens and facilities that celebrate the world of plants and flowers that surrounds us. The park has a Texas native trail, greenhouse, conservatory, and bird watching stations.

Giant Chairs *(above and left)*

Using plans from Alabama, garden volunteers built huge Adirondack chairs and a matching picnic table as a bit of colorful whimsy. The huge lawn chairs overlook a lawn chess game in the San Antonio Botanical Garden amphitheater. Flora in context builds an appreciation for the plant life that surrounds us.

Indoors and Out

San Antonio is temperate, almost tropical, but the Botanical Garden can't grow examples of all of the Earth's flora without a few controlled environment greenhouse facilities. The Lucille Halsell Conservatory includes special collections in a desert room, tropical and palm pavilions, and a room for special exhibits.

UTSA *(above)*

The University of Texas at San Antonio was founded in 1969 and its first president had an office in HemisFair Park. Students attended classes in an office center until 1975, when the main campus opened. Today, the university offers 162 degree programs to 28,787 students taught by 1,383 faculty members.

Our Lady of the Lake University *(opposite)*

With roots in its Catholic missions, San Antonio welcomed Sisters for Divine Providence when they arrived in Texas in 1866. They founded a school for women, which added college classes in 1911, become coeducational by 1969, and added University to its name in 1975. More than 3,000 students attend 57 degree programs.

St. Anthony de Padua

Named for San Antonio's patron, St. Anthony parish started as a mission of service in 1927. Placed in Cementville, a small chapel was built by cement workers and pecan shellers. The current building, resembling the Alamo, was built in 1957.

St. Anthony de Padua

The patron saint of lost things was born in Portugal and served in Morocco. Illness caused him to travel home, but his ship was diverted to Sicily. Eventually, he served the small town of Forti, Romagna, where he became known as a forceful preacher with a deep knowledge of scripture.

Basilica of the National Shrine of the Little Flower (opposite)

The first shrine to Sister Thérèse outside France, San Antonio's Basilica was completed in 1931. St. Thérèse Province of the Discalced Carmelite Friars in San Antonio staff the church, which has a school across the street and serves San Antonio's near Westside.

La Veladora of Our Lady of Guadalupe (above)

Here, she is known as La Virgen, who appeared to Juan Diego and assured him of God's blessing for his people, the Aztecs. A veladora is a votive candle, often sold in botanicas, and lit to enhance prayers for intercession. Jesse Treviño created the 3D ceramic mural.

The Saga (*above*)

In 2014, the Main Plaza Commission, with cooperation from the Archdiocese of San Antonio, unveiled a massive multimedia presentation projected on the façade of San Fernando Cathedral. Produced by French artist Xavier de Richemont, the 24-minute presentation tells the story of San Antonio nearly every night in Main Plaza.

San Fernando Cathedral (*opposite*)

Fifteen Canary Island families established San Fernando Cathedral five years before the mission church was built at the Alamo, making it the first church in San Antonio and the oldest cathedral in Texas. Legend claims that bones in a tomb built into the church belonged to heroes of the Alamo.

Day of the Dead (above and left)

San Antonio celebrates Halloween just like any other city, but two days later, an equally festive tradition, Día de los Muertos, is celebrated when the deceased are remembered. People dress as skeletons to portray an exciting afterlife, and gather at La Villita (above), El Mercado (left), and other venues throughout the city.

Luminaria Arts Festival (*above*)

Luminaria is a relatively new festival in San Antonio, initiated in 2008. The event is a nighttime multi-genre celebration with music, art installations, poetry, theatre, film, dance, and fun. Similar night festivals in Paris and Madrid inspired Luminaria, which uses art to cast light into the darkness.

Diwali Light Festival (*right*)

One of the largest festivals in India, San Antonio's Diwali is the only event of its kind in America. The festival draws 15,000 visitors to shop at a large variety of vendor booths, to see Diya Floats, fireworks, and performing arts, and to eat Indian cuisine.

117

Dancers! *(above and left)*

Folklorico dancers are part of nearly every celebration in San Antonio. All summer long, Fiesta Noche del Rio fills the Arneson River Theatre on the River Walk, with benches lining the edge of La Villita. Since 1957, songs and dances from Argentina, Spain, Mexico, and Texas have been performed here.

Fiesta San Antonio *(opposite)*

Just a few weeks after winter releases its grip, San Antonio busts loose for 17 days. More than 100 nonprofit groups organize thousands of people to stage parades, Night In Old San Antonio, King William Fair, Charreada, and other major events. Food vendors, King Antonio and Rey Feo, Fiesta Queens, bands, and more punctuate the festivities.

San Antonio Zoo

(above and opposite)

Merchant and philanthropist George Brackenridge once kept exotic animals on his estate north of downtown San Antonio, and today the park he gave to his adopted city features a world-class zoo. The 35-acre zoo has more than 3,500 animals from 750 species. The zoo celebrated its centennial in 2014.

San Antonio Charros Association

(above and left)

Three centuries before American settlers brought cows and cowboys to
Texas, horseback caballeros wrangled
cattle. Haciendas hosted competitions
where caballeros could impress señori-
tas with riding and roping skills. San
Antonio is home to the oldest sanctioned
Charros Association in the United States.

A Family Affair *(above and right)*

Charreada is an elaborate, multi-generational effort. Participants train all year and invest in authentic costumes. Silver accessories shine off shirts, boots, hats, and tack. Women have their own events, escaramuza, where they recreate daring rides of the revolution, creating great clouds of dust as decoys to confuse soldiers.

Rodeo *(above, right, and opposite)*

Charreada gave birth to American rodeo. In February, Stock Show & Rodeo fills the city. Amateur and professional riders alike compete in a variety of traditional events, a large carnival surrounds Freeman Coliseum, longhorns parade downtown, youngsters present show animals, and lively music fills the air.

Alamodome

Home to the San Antonio Spurs for a decade, the Alamodome is a multi-use arena that can be configured for football, basketball, hockey, entertainment, or convention facilities. Located just east of HemisFair, the arena's current principal tenant is the UTSA Roadrunners.

AT&T Center (top)

Perennial NBA leaders, the San Antonio Spurs play in AT&T Center, built for the team by Bexar County. The AT&T Center is also used for major concerts, autocross, and other events. In February, the Spurs take an annual "rodeo road trip" as the Stock Show & Rodeo takes over the facility.

Freeman Coliseum (bottom)

The original home of the Stock Show & Rodeo, the Freeman Coliseum can seat up to 11,000 for large events. It is named for Joe & Harry Freeman, who earned their fortune in cotton, oil, and automobile dealerships. Like many San Antonians, they were weekend ranchers.

Al Rendon is San Antonio's photographer. From landmarks to community leaders, Al has photographed the face and heart of San Antonio. He has also operated fine art galleries, and his exhibitions have traveled the world. His photographs have filled books about the history of Fiesta, Charreada, and Red McCombs' fine silver collection. Al is both craftsman and artist. His commercial photography crafts excellent images for executive portraiture, architectural documentation, and marketing. Al's art photography spans San Antonio's culture. In the 1980s, he served as official photographer for the Guadalupe Cultural Arts Center, the Fiesta Commission, and for many years, has provided editorial use photography to the Convention & Visitor's Bureau. In 2011, Al was one of six photographers chosen to represent San Antonio at the International Photographic Art Exhibition in Lishui City, China. His archival prints are in the Smithsonian National Portrait Gallery and American Art Museum, Museum of Fine Art in Houston, the Cattle Raisers Museum in Fort Worth, and the Mexican American Museum of Art in Chicago. For more information, see www.AlRendon.com.

A San Antonio copywriter, **Gary S. Whitford** specializes in non-profit marketing and the arts. He has edited two books by Juanita Chipman that compile the writings of women in the family of Dr. Ferdinand Herff, a German surgeon that came to San Antonio with the Turnverein movement. Gary grew up in Wichita, Kansas and arrived in San Antonio in 1970. He has worked as a newspaper editor, publications specialist, multimedia director and, for most of his career, freelancer.

Al Rendon and Gary have worked together on various projects for more than 30 years. From a long poem with 28 images called *Fragile, Romance*, to exhibit concepts and other business support, Gary has always been "Al's writer."

Gary has two children and three grandchildren. He lives with his partner and two dachshunds on the Northside.